IMAGES
of Sport

GREENOCK MORTON FOOTBALL CLUB 1874-1999

The Morton FC crest of 1971.

IMAGES
of Sport

GREENOCK MORTON FOOTBALL CLUB 1874-1999

Compiled by
Jim Jeffrey

TEMPUS

First published 1999
Copyright © Jim Jeffrey, 1999

Tempus Publishing Limited
The Mill, Brimscombe Port,
Stroud, Gloucestershire, GL5 2QG

ISBN 0 7524 1803 3

Typesetting and origination by
Tempus Publishing Limited
Printed in Great Britain by
Midway Clark Printing, Wiltshire

Contents

Foreword

It was a considerable compliment when Greenock Morton Football Club invited me to compile this photographic record on their behalf. Having been involved with their match programme for almost a decade, I had built up a strong feeling for the club and knew that it meant so much to so many people that I liked. The daunting task was to somehow capture over a century of drama in just over 100 pages.

The club's past was memorably and quite superbly put on record in 1974 when the then club secretary Tom Robertson compiled a loving history of the club. I have deliberately tried to avoid repeating the materials Tom compiled twenty-five years ago. My aim from the outset was to cover new areas and more importantly bring the history of Morton up to date. The quarter-century since Tom's book came out has been quite eventful and if this publication can be viewed in tandem with Tom's history then I would consider my task a success.

Morton are one of Scotland's oldest provincial clubs and one of the best loved. The people of Greenock, Port Glasgow and Gourock have supported the club with a passion few other supporters can match. They deserve praise as it would have been all too easy to jump on a bus and zoom along the M8 to watch Celtic or Rangers and enjoy some success. It only takes a promotion push or a big cup-tie to show the support base Morton has.

The last century has given Morton supporters a series of ups and downs, here's hoping the next century gives them more of the former and less of the latter.

Acknowledgements

Many people have helped me in the compilation of this photographic history of Morton. I am very grateful to them, not only for the loan of materials but for the sheer enthusiasm they had for the project and their desire to share rare items with other Morton supporters.

Gary Miller was the man who suggested I tackle the project on the club's behalf and he supplied a wealth of old programmes to get me started. A splendid ambassador for the club, he meets every request with a cheeriness which typifies those who work at Cappielow Park.

John Borthwick, a local programme expert, greatly expanded the items at my disposal and was a source of many good ideas. Without the services of local photographer Kenny Ramsay, the recent history of Morton Football Club would be less well documented than it is. Kenny has braved all sorts of elements to capture images at Cappielow Park and his genuine love of for his local club shines through in his marvellous pictures.

Perhaps the main privilege of writing the Morton programme over these last few years has been dealing with the remarkable and much-loved Arthur Montford. Arthur is a veritable encyclopaedia on the club, and his help was much appreciated as was that of another contender for the title of 'Mr Morton ', former player and manager Allan McGraw. Allan is one of the game's great gentlemen and was an enormous help in compiling the section on the Scandinavian players.

Gilbert McCracken has supported the club since boyhood, as his father and grandfather have done before, and many of the older items in this collection belong to him. A constant source of inspiration, it would not surprise me to learn that Gilbert's family have blue and white blood in their veins.

My good friends at the *Sunday Post* came up with a host of photographs and I must thank editor David Walker who has always shown a willingness to help when I have mentioned the words 'Greenock Morton'.

Finally, I would like to finish by thanking my wife, Kath, for putting up with my turning the living room into a virtual shrine to Greenock Morton over the last few months.

Kevin Thomas celebrates a goal for Morton at St Mirren in the late 1990s.

Introduction

Greenock Morton Football Club was founded in 1874 and has played at Cappielow Park since 1897 in what is by any standards a lengthy tenancy. The first club in Scotland to form itself into a public limited company, Morton were always keen to make progress. By 1899 Cappielow was the best-appointed ground in Renfrewshire, and top class cycling and athletics events took place at the stadium.

The club name has often attracted questions and by common consent it believed to derive from the founding fathers of the club who lived locally in a street named Morton Terrace. That street, in turn, was probably named after a local provost. At various times in the history of the club the names Morton and Greenock Morton have been preferred.

By the start of the Second World War, Morton had won the Scottish Cup and been promoted twice; moreover a number of their players had achieved international status. However, harder times have followed in the post-war era and the good times have come in fairly thin servings.

Morton lifted the Scottish Cup for the only time in their history back in 1922 when they defeated the highly-fancied Rangers. The Glasgow side were hot-favourites particularly when Morton had to do without the services of their ace-marksman George French on final day. However, a goal directly from a free-kick by Jimmy Gourlay won the day and sent Greenock into celebration mode. In 1948 the same two sides again contested the final with the Glasgow club gaining revenge, albeit after a replay. Three times Morton have come close to emulating those cup highs, but semi-final defeats to Hearts, Celtic and Rangers in 1968, 1969 and 1981 have thwarted them.

The Scottish Cup was not contested in the war years, but alternative tournaments were organised. In season 1914/15 a War Shield was played for and Morton won the final, beating the mighty Rangers 2-1 to do so. One of their goal-scorers was Stan Seymour, who was later to earn great fame with Newcastle United. Seymour was but the first of some truly famous players to represent Morton.

Since 1948 Morton have relied largely on visits to play Queen's Park for trips to Hampden Park but in 1964 they did contest the League Cup Final only to fall heavily to Rangers who scored five times without reply. They reached that final by beating Hibernian in the semi-final with Allan McGraw scoring the penalty winner in a replay at Ibrox. There have been further League Cup Semi-final appearances since then but Celtic, twice, and Aberdeen scuppered their hopes.

Glamorous as the cups are, it is the League upon which clubs are normally judged, and Morton, alas, has yet to land the Championship. Indeed, excitement for Morton has tended to centre around promotion and relegation jousts rather than genuine championship aspirations.

First relegated in 1927, Morton took only two seasons to bounce back, but demotion was not always so swiftly rectified. In 1952 they went down and took over a decade to bounce back. The catalyst to Morton's halcyon days of the 1960s was a remarkable man by the name of Hal Stewart. Had Hal been active in football today he would have revelled in the title of 'Director of Football'. His enthusiasm for Morton and Greenock was insatiable and he orchestrated a root and branch restructuring of the club. In came a flood of Scandinavian players, in came brightly designed jerseys, and in came success. Two promotions were the highlight of Hal Stewart's era, along with several cup exploits.

In the early 1970s Morton seemed to slip into decline but the arrival of Benny Rooney as manager rekindled the flames of passion at Cappielow Park. In 1978 he orchestrated their promotion and subsequent survival in the Premier Division. Not until 1983 did they go down and this set in train a remarkable piece of yo-yo activity. In 1984 they went up, in '85 back down, in '87 back up and in 1988 down again. One thing emerges from Morton's League record – with ten relegations to their name they are not a predictable side.

In April 1936 Morton played Raith Rovers and a forward by the name of John Calder made history by netting eight goals, a Scottish League record (which remarkably was equalled by a Raith Rovers player just over a year later). In terms of consistent scoring in a season the much-loved Allan McGraw holds the Morton record, being credited with 58 goals in season 1963/64.

Some magnificent players have worn the blue and white of Morton, although strictly speaking the most famous of them all wore yellow. The man in question was the magnificent goalkeeper Jimmy Cowan who went on to win twenty-five caps for Scotland. How ironic that he should have been signed on a free transfer from fierce local rivals St Mirren.

Outfield stars who have shone at Cappielow include Joe Jordan, father and son Tommy and Neil Orr, Billy Steel, Joe McLaughlin, Mark McGhee, Neil Mochan, Neil McNab, and the sensational Andy Ritchie. In the modern game all would be worth huge sums, but Ritchie was probably priceless!

Finally Morton are indeed a club of innovations. They experimented with fluorescent orange jerseys in the sixties and had a fan who accompanied every Morton attack with a blast on his bugle. In the same era they brought over Scandinavian footballers by the barrowload. Much of that foresight belonged to the vision of the aforementioned chairman Hal Stewart, who shook Scottish football with his drive and energy. Hal Stewart, Jimmy Cowan, Andy Ritchie, Allan McGraw … Morton fans have never been short of personalities.

I started this introduction with a brief reference to Cappielow Park and Morton's extraordinary lengthy tenancy there. Sadly, as this book prepared to go to press the very future of that old ground was in doubt. No longer a suitable venue for top class football it had one last hurrah when Celtic called for a Scottish Cup Quarter-final tie in 1999. When the next book on Greenock Morton is published the author will hopefully be able to start with the story of a new stadium.

One

The Early Days ...
Relegation and the Riot

Even before winning the Scottish Cup in 1922, Morton were making quite a name for themselves. Granted League status in 1893 they were in the top league for the start of the twentieth century. Fortunately, in the early days of League football, relegation was not automatic and clubs were elected rather than promoted to the top flight. Thus Morton had time to find their feet.

By 1912 they had finished a best ever sixth in the League, and were fourth in both 1914 and 1915 before finishing third in 1916 behind the Old Firm. The inability to wrest the title away from the Glasgow giants clearly rankled the home support and when Celtic came to Cappielow in 1922 seeking to land the title it was too much to take for some Morton supporters – the infamous 'Cappielow Riot' ensued.

The 1922 Cup success should be viewed therefore in the context of a steadily improving provincial side. Unfortunately, Morton were unable to follow up on the Cup success and in 1927 they were relegated for the first time. This was hardly surprising as that season's results had included an 8-2 home defeat to Rangers and several six-goal thrashings away from home.

Calamity struck as the club struggled to adapt to life in Division Two and finished third bottom. What caused the transformation that followed may never be known, but in 1929 Morton were second in Division Two and were promoted.

Above: A Morton line-up in 1920. From left to right, back row: R. Brown, R. McGregor, D. Edwards, J. Buchanan, J. Wright, M. Watt, W. Gibson. Front row: A. McNab, J. Gourlay, P. Thorp and R. McKay. In the background the terracing is uncovered and less steeply banked than today but the building in the background was to survive for a further seventy years!

Above: McNab, Gourlay and French were an essential part of the Morton side that won the Scottish Cup in 1922.

Below: Edwards, Wright and McIntyre played their part too. These pictures come from a Morton handbook of the early 1920s.

Below opposite: The proud Scottish Cup winners. In April 1922 Morton landed the trophy for the only time in their history. They beat Vale of Leithen, Clydebank, Clyde, Motherwell and Aberdeen en route to the final where they overcame Rangers 1-0. The crucial goal was scored by Jimmy Gourlay. Photographed from left to right, back row: M. Watt, J. Hempsey, P. Thorpe, W. Gibson. Middle row: J. Henry, D. Campbell, J. Gourlay, R. McGregor, J. Wright, J. McIntyre, D. Edwards, R. Brown, R. Cochran, H. Howatt. Front row: R. Adam, R. McKay, J. Buchanan, Provost W. McMillan, G. French, A. Brown, J. Campbell. Seated in front: A. McNab, J. McMinn. George French scored nine goals before the final but missed out on the big day through injury.

A team group from the 1925/26 season. From left to right, back row: Hunter, Hyslop, Fotheringham, Jessiman, Moir, Buchanan. Front row: Wilson, Brown, Orr, French, Gourlay.

Legendary trainer Hugh Howatt tells an enthusiastic audience the tale of Morton's cup triumph several years after the event. Note the picket fence on the new Cappielow Main Stand.

A group of players sample a cup of tea on the Cappielow pitch. Clearly visible is the basic nature of the terracing at the Wee Dublin End of the Greenock ground.

Measuring for new boots before the season.

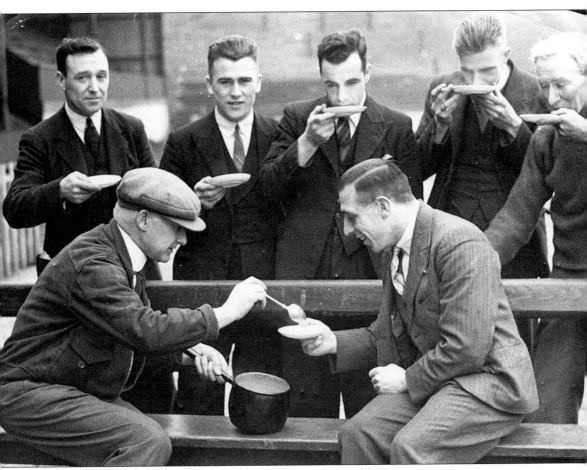

A rich broth! Hugh Howatt is on the extreme right of this picture as spoons run out at Cappielow.

Winger Colin Liddell was born in Glasgow in June 1925. A pupil of Albert Secondary School in Glasgow, he joined Queen's Park and was a key player in the 'Spiders' side before signing for Morton in 1947. During the war he had played for the RAF and attracted the interest of several clubs. Tall and strong, he was typical of many post-war wingers, of whom Rangers legendary Willie Waddell was the brightest example. Gone for a spell were the diminutive tanner-ba' players. In June 1949 he signed for Hearts in a transfer that added £10,000 to the Cappielow bank balance and cost Hearts a club-record fee. However, despite the huge price tag, he failed to settle at Tynecastle and two years later was on the move again, this time to Rangers in a swop deal that took Eddie Rutherford to Edinburgh. He fared better initially at Ibrox and kept the talented Johnny Hubbard confined to the sidelines. In 1955 Colin returned to Morton to bring the curtain down on his career. He travelled to the Far East after leaving Morton for a second time and is reported as having played in Singapore. He died in 1997 in Kilmarnock.

Two
The Hungry Thirties and Forties

Morton experienced the full range of football emotions in the thirties. They began the decade in the top division and after three near things were duly relegated in the 1933 season. In 1936 they were pipped for promotion by local rivals St Mirren despite racking up an 11-2 home win over Raith Rovers in which Calder ran riot and scored eight times – a Scottish record. The derby game at Love Street went into local folklore as Morton bravely lost 5-4, a defeat that was to prove costly come the final reckoning.

Despite the set backs Morton bounced back and were promoted in 1937 only to be instantly relegated. The 1937/38 season was disastrous, particularly the 5 February meeting with St Mirren … ending as it did in a humiliating 7-0 reversal. The 1938/39 season was one of frustration for travelling fans. On no fewer than three occasions Morton lost away games 6-5; East Fife, Forfar and Kings Park being the opponents in high-scoring affairs.

After four games in the 1939/40 season the Second World War broke out with Morton supporters' appetite for success very much unfulfilled.

Upon the resumption of normal footballing activities Morton were able to hold their own. Indeed, in 1948 they reached the Scottish Cup Final only to lose to Rangers in a replay. Over 250,000 people watched the two games! In typical Morton fashion they followed this cup epic up by being relegated within twelve months. That said they were very unlucky to meet and lose to a title chasing Rangers in a key game in late April.

Just how unlucky Morton had been was emphasised in the summer of 1950 as they roared straight back to the top league.

Little did the club know it but relegation was just around the corner. Still, this match programme from season 1930/31 was from happier times when visits to the likes of Celtic were still very much part of the annual fixture list. Match programmes were relatively rare in this era and the issue here is one of the oldest featuring Morton.

Match programmes were so rare in Scotland in the 1930s that the same design, and indeed printer, was utilized by more than one club. St Bernard's were an Edinburgh based side and tricky opponents on their own ground, but Morton won this game 1-0 in 1935.

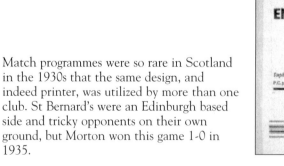

In season 1936/37 Morton ended their four year Second Division exile by gaining promotion. The men who took Morton back to the top flight were from left to right, back row: Baird, Maley, Stewart, Simpson, Mooney, Robb. Front row: Collins, Benzie, Black, Smith, McGarry, Howatt (Coach).

Jimmy Davies was appointed Morton manager in 1939. He brought Billy Campbell (centre) to the club, and more importantly goalkeeping sensation Jimmy Cowan. In season 1941/42 he steered the club to the Southern League Cup Final and eclipsed that by taking Morton to the 1948 Scottish Cup Final. On the extreme right of the photograph is Jimmy Gourlay, who had scored the goal that won the Scottish Cup in 1922.

A team group from the 1946/47 season: From left to right, back row: Davies (Manager), Westwater, Maley, Campbell, Aird, McFeat, Fyfe, Kelly, Whyte, Gourlay (Trainer). Front row: McKillop, Cupples, Neil, Garth, McGarry, McInnes.

Morton began issuing programmes for fixtures at Cappielow Park in the years after the war. This issue is from season 1947/48 and is for a game against Falkirk, although that information is not printed on the cover. What is on the cover are details of the forthcoming fixtures and a huge advert for Aitken's Falkirk Beer, a common advert in football programmes up and down Scotland.

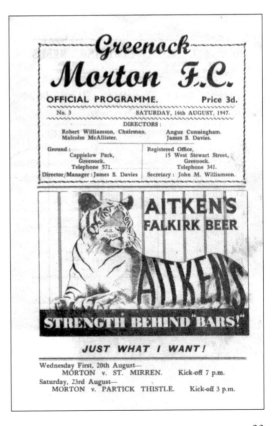

David Cupples in 1947. A tricky striker, he was Morton's centre forward in the 1948 Cup Final. He was signed on a free transfer from Partick Thistle and later served Hamilton.

A busy Cappielow looks on as Morton's 1947/48 team photograph is taken. From left to right, back row: Mitchell, Whigham, Cowan, Campbell, Miller, Whyte. Front row: Hepburn, McGarrity, Cupples, Orr, Liddell. This team would steer Morton to the Scottish Cup Final in April 1948.

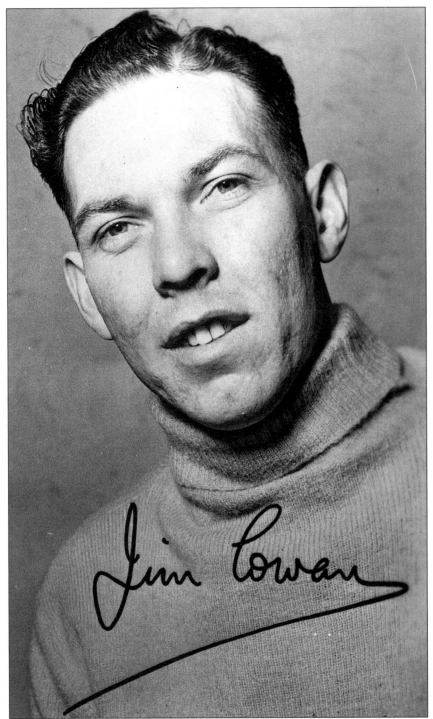

Goalkeeper Jimmy Cowan joined Morton on a free transfer from St Mirren during the Second World War and went on to establish himself as the greatest-ever Morton player. He won twenty-five Scotland caps and his agility and bravery made him a national hero. He stayed with Morton until 1953 when he signed for Sunderland for the then considerable sum of £8,000.

The famous English internationalist Stanley Matthews played for Morton several times during the war. Matthews joined the RAF during the war and was stationed in Blackpool, but played as a guest when on leave for several clubs including Rangers, Airdrie and Morton. He played in the New Year massacre of St Mirren in 1943, laying on the bulk of Crum's six goals in the 8-0 win. Later, the legendary Tommy Lawton joined him in the Morton ranks.

Morton Juniors was a brave attempt by Morton to groom the finest local youth for footballing success with Morton.

Billy Steel was with Morton in the late 1940s as a part-time player working in Denny Town Hall during the day. He was eventually sold to Derby County for a record fee of £15,500. Billy had joined Morton when only seventeen and was capped by Scotland before leaving Cappielow. An inside left, he played with considerable skill and when Dundee bought him from Derby County for £23,000 it was a record fee for a Scottish club.

In 1948 Morton almost repeated their Scottish Cup Final success of 1921. This time, however, Rangers turned the tables and took the trophy, but only after a replay.

The replay programme is extremely rare and rather cruelly shows a Morton player scoring a goal, the irony of which was not lost on the Greenock support who witnessed a 1-0 defeat.

The Morton club crest captures the maritime theme of the club perfectly with a boat and rope displayed prominently. The club crest has been tinkered with over the years but the arrival of the centenary saw the basic themes remaining the same.

Three
The Fifties

The decade started with Morton back in the top flight – but that didn't last long. When the 1950/51 season had seen Morton lose 8-0 at Tynecastle it was clear the defence was not all it could be. Yet, when the club were demoted in 1951/52, it was another very unlucky relegation. This time no fewer than eight clubs (half of the league!) were struggling to avoid joining Stirling Albion in Division Two. Morton ultimately went down as cup finalists Motherwell won a key game 2-0 at Cappielow when really their mind should have been on more pressing matters!

Mid-table Second Division mediocrity followed, with the 1950s giving no sign of any success at all. There was no joy on the cup front either with Morton unable to register a single appearance in the Scottish Cup Quarter-finals. The League Cup, by now well established, offered little relief either. In 1952 Morton did reach the quarter-finals but were shown how far they had fallen by a ruthless Hibernian side that scored six in each of the two legs to register a thumping 12-3 aggregate defeat.

The remarkable Jimmy Cowan is helpless here to prevent Rangers scoring at Cappielow. Also in the picture is defender Whigham, whom Morton had signed from Queen's Park.

This time Cowan foils Rangers, looking on are Mitchell, Whigham and Hunter.

With the exception of 1950 to 1952, Morton spent the 1950s rooted in the Second Division. Indeed throughout the fifties Morton were unable in any season to win more than half of their League games. The Scottish Cup was a source of constant pain too with a day out at Hampden never anything more than a distant pipe dream. This team was unable to break the depression settling in over Greenock. From left to right, back row: Murney, Anderson, Wylie, Kay, Hinshelwood, Swanson. Front row: McGill, Gourlay, Beaton, McAllister, Phillips.

Pictured with Tom McGarrity (left), Neil Mochan was one of the finest Morton forwards in the immediate post-war era. Born in Larbert in 1927, Neil Mochan joined Morton in 1944 and proved himself a great signing. An outside left of power and pace he was a prolific marksman and was eventually sold to Middlesbrough in 1951, having proved himself a most popular figure in Greenock. When he came back to Scotland it was to join Celtic and in truth he never looked back.

The drain of talent to the North-East of England continued two years later when goalkeeper Jimmy Cowan joined Sunderland. Cowan was one goalkeeper of whom even the English media could find little fault.

A profile of Billy Campbell from a Morton programme of the era.

BILLY CAMPBELL BENEFIT GAME

St. Mirren League Select

versus

Greenock Morton
(PAST AND PRESENT)

At IBROX STADIUM, GLASGOW,
(Ground kindly granted by Rangers F.C.)

On WEDNESDAY, 23rd AUGUST, 1950.

PROGRAMME, - - - PRICE 3d.

Ibrox Stadium is the home of Rangers. However, in 1950 the Glasgow club kindly allowed Morton to use it for a testimonial match in aid of Billy Campbell. The opposition was local rivals St Mirren, although, as the cover reveals, neither side was a strict selection from the current pool of players.

The men who carried Morton's hopes in the1951/52 season. From left to right, back row: Little, Mitchell, Cowan, Batton, Whigham, Hunter. Front row: Gibson, Garth, Linwood, McGarrity, McVinish.

A reunion in the 1960s of the men who helped win the Scottish Cup in 1922. Pictured here, from left to right: Bobby McGregor, Bobby Brown, Jimmy Gourlay, Jock McIntyre and Alex McMinn.

Four

The Swinging Sixties

To support Morton in the 1960s was the equivalent of enjoying a roller-coaster ride. Looking back it seems hard to imagine that the 1960/61 season ended with Morton bottom of the entire Scottish League structure, having collected only 21 points from 36 Second Division games.

In came a new owner in the shape of Hal Stewart and the rest is, as they say, history. In 1962 Morton finished third in the Second Division, a position they repeated in 1963, but this time they lost out on promotion by a single point.

What followed in the 1963/64 season still amazes. Morton won the Second Division by collecting maximum points in no fewer than 32 of their 36 League games. They scored 135 goals, Allan McGraw alone netting 58 for the season. There was also the small matter of reaching the League Cup Final.

Inspired now by a tidal wave of local emotion, Morton survived in the First Division with ease, welcomed a growing colony of Scandinavian players and reached the League Cup Semi-final.

Perhaps it was too much too soon. In 1966 Morton were relegated. However, that was a mere stutter and promotion was won instantly with 113 goals being scored. This time they went on to finish sixth in the top league and reach the Scottish Cup Semi-finals. The decade drew to a close with Per Bartram scoring a ten minute hat-trick at Celtic Park and another Scottish Cup Semi-final being contested.

Rarely had a decade that promised so little delivered so much!

Hal Stewart was deservedly known as 'Mr Morton'. He joined the club in 1961, which had been in the doldrums since relegation in 1952. He quickly brought experienced professionals Archie Robertson and Doug Cowie to the club, while his next masterstroke was the introduction of a clutch of Scandinavian players. A successful youth policy that brought the likes of Joe Harper and Joe Jordan to the club also helped. He often wore a hat and is pictured here with Benny Rooney, chairman Hugh Currie and assistant manager Mike Jackson.

Morton in unusual white tops with blue satin silk shorts. The players in the photograph are from left to right, back row: John Campbell, John Hart, Ian Couper, Hugh Murray, James Kiernan, ? Cunningham. Front row: Billy Gray, Jim Frizzell, Billy Collins, John Brown, Brian Callan.

Centre forward Joe Caven had a big impact on Morton in the 1960s. Although rather on the short side, he proved himself to be a tough and reliable player. Signed from Raith Rovers in 1963, he had previously played in England with Brighton and Hove Albion.

'Shirts and Ties'. Allan McGraw(left) with a Morton colleague. McGraw was signed from army football in 1961 but had played with Renfrew Juniors before doing his National Service duties. Morton would fly him home from Germany in his early days. He was quite simply a prolific marksman and in season 1963/64 scored 58 goals, grabbing 10 in the space of four days when he hit five in back-to-back games against Brechin City and Hamilton Accies. He was eventually sold to Hibernian in 1967 but by that stage had begun to suffer from the knee problems that would hamper him in later life. He came back to work on the coaching staff in 1970 and was appointed manager in 1985.

In the 1963/64 season, Morton stormed out of the Second Division breaking a string of records in the process. Of 36 League games no fewer than 32 were won and only one lost. The team scored a remarkable 135 goals and at one stage had 23 consecutive League wins to boast of. The side also reached the League Cup Final. This team picture from early in the season shows from left to right, back row: John Boyd, Jimmy Mallon, Ian Millar, Jim Reilly, Jim Kiernan, Hugh Strachan. Front row: Bobby Campbell, Maurice Stevenson, Joe Caven, Allan McGraw, Jimmy Wilson.

Morton celebrated with the traditional lap of honour when promotion was clinched. As this photograph clearly shows, the bulk of the crowd stayed back to show their appreciation.

Following the lap of honour it was time to pose for photographs, with those who missed the actual ninety minutes not being left out of things.

Toasting success: the victorious Morton side celebrate promotion in the Cappielow dressing room.

Coach Bobby Howitt joins the celebrations. From left to right are: Boyd, Kiernan, Reilly, Campbell, Mallon, Adamson, McGraw, Brown, Wilson, Byrne and Howitt.

Snow in the winter of 1967 considerably reduced the gate at this Morton match. The goalmouths have been cleared and an orange ball is called into service.

The giant crane in Ratho Street was a feature of the Greenock landscape in the mid-1960s. Here is the view it afforded of Cappielow.

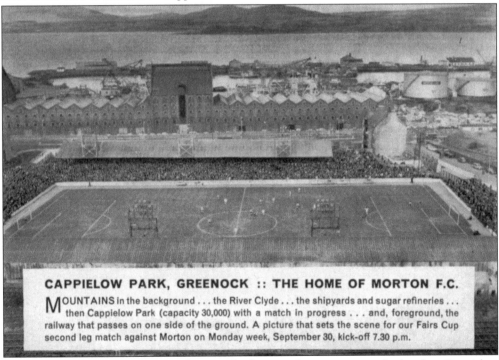

CAPPIELOW PARK, GREENOCK :: THE HOME OF MORTON F.C.

MOUNTAINS in the background . . . the River Clyde . . . the shipyards and sugar refineries . . . then Cappielow Park (capacity 30,000) with a match in progress . . . and, foreground, the railway that passes on one side of the ground. A picture that sets the scene for our Fairs Cup second leg match against Morton on Monday week, September 30, kick-off 7.30 p.m.

Cappielow in the mid-1960s. The aerial photograph captures perfectly the Cappielow atmosphere. The distant hills, the River Clyde and the shipyards all combine to give Morton a ground steeped in the fabric of the West of Scotland.

The sixties were not all 'sweetness and light' and relegation took Morton back to the Second Division. Here Morton are in stripes and defending stoutly at Stirling Albion's Annfield. The Morton number five is Dane, John Madsen, who was later sold to Hibernian.

Maccabi Tel Aviv toured Scotland in 1966 and played Morton as well as Hearts. Here the Israeli players relax after the August fixture at Cappielow.

'Britain's Best Dressed Team'. Morton's squad get together for a night out. From left to right, back row: Morris Stevenson, Joe Caven, Ian Miller, Jackie McGuigan, Hugh Strachan, Bobby Campbell. Middle row: Jim Keirnan, Jim Reilly, Allan McGraw, Jimmy Mallon, John Boyd. Seated on the ground: Jim Wilson.

The name in the background says it all! Morton pictured in pin stripes before a match at Cappielow. From left to right, back row: Wilson, Boyd, -?-, Brown, Keirnan, Strachan, -?-. Front row: Adamson, Stevenson, Caven, McGraw, Byrne.

A similar strip but this time with heavier stripes. Here, the team is pictured with the Renfrewshire Cup.

In 1967 Morton won the Renfrewshire Cup. The Morton Quiz team of Strachan, Eric Smith, Murray and McLean are doubtless grateful that the photographer did not require the trophy held aloft!

46

Jorn Sorensen (10) is on target here as Morton score against Hamilton Accies at Cappielow. The distinctive factory roofs behind the goal have long since gone.

Morton in the mid-1960s had some exciting new talent emerging, particularly young striker Joe Harper. From left to right, back row: -?-, Harper, -?-, Stevenson, Adams. Middle row: -?-, -?-, -?- , Laughlin, Sorensen, Boyd, Mallon, Strachan, -?-, Howitt (coach). Front row -?-, Johansen, -?- , Caven, McGraw, Wilson, -?-.

Morton also attracted healthy gates up and down Scotland in the 1960s, as this big crowd at Hibernian's Easter Road shows. Smith is the Morton marksman in this picture. The old Easter Road half-time scoreboard is just visible to the right of the Hibs goalkeeper.

Another goal for pint-sized striker Joe Harper. Joe was perhaps the cream of the crop in terms of Morton's youth policy. A marvellous little striker he had two spells with Morton sandwiched around a stint with Huddersfield Town. After his second period with Morton he went on to star with Aberdeen, Everton and Hibernian, as well as Scotland.

Scottish League Cup

		F.	A.
Aug. 10—Ayr United	(A)	1	0
„ 14—Stranraer	(H)	5	0
„ 17—Clyde	(H)	3	1
„ 24—Ayr United	(H)	5	2
„ 28—Stranraer	(A)	2	1
„ 31—Clyde	(A)	4	0
Sept. 11—Motherwell	(A)	0	0
„ 18—Motherwell	(H)	2	0

SEMI FINAL—

Oct. 7—Hibernian	(A)	1	1
„ 14—Hibernian	(A)	1	0

FINAL—

Oct. 26—Rangers	(A)	0	5

Scottish League Division II

		F.	A.
Aug. 21—Stranraer	(A)	3	1
Sept. 4—Dumbarton	(H)	5	1
„ 7—Ayr United	(H)	2	0
„ 14—Stenhousemuir	(A)	5	4
„ 21—Free Day			
„ 25—Brechin City	(A)	7	3
„ 28—Clyde	(A)	2	1
Oct. 1—Brechin City	(H)	8	1
„ 5—East Fife	(H)	6	1
„ 12—Montrose	(A)	2	0
„ 19—Berwick Rangers ...	(H)	7	1

Nov. 2—Forfar	(A)	6	4
„ 4—Hamilton	(H)	8	0
„ 9—Stirling Albion	(H)	5	1
„ 16—Queen's Park	(H)	4	0
„ 23—Arbroath	(A)	2	1
„ 30—Alloa	(A)	3	0
Dec. 7—Albion Rovers	(H)	3	1
„ 14—Cowdenbeath	(H)	2	0
„ 21—Raith Rovers	(A)	3	0
„ 28—Stranraer	(H)	4	0
Jan. 1—Ayr United	(A)	3	1
„ 2—Stenhousemuir	(H)	7	2
„ 4—Free Day			
„ 18—Clyde	(H)	3	0
Feb. 1—East Fife	(A)	1	3
„ 8—Montrose	(H)	2	0
„ 15—Berwick Rangers ...	(A)	3	1
„ 22—Hamilton	(A)	3	1
„ 29—Forfar	(H)	6	1
Mar. 7—Stirling Albion	(A)	2	1
„ 14—Queen's Park	(A)	3	0
„ 21—Arbroath	(H)	2	2
„ 28—Alloa	(H)	2	2
Apr. 4—Albion Rovers	(A)	0	0
„ 18—Cowdenbeath	(A)	5	1
„ 25—Raith Rovers	(H)	4	2

Summer Cup

	P	W	L	D	F	A	Pts
Partick Th.	5	3	2	0	13	7	6
Morton	5	2	1	2	6	4	6
St. Mirren ...	5	2	2	1	3	5	5
Th. Lanark	5	1	3	1	8	14	3

In 1963/64 Morton swept all before them as the list of results reveals. Twice Morton scored eight goals in a League game, three times they hit the 'heavenly seven', and they rattled in six on three occasions. 135 goals were scored in just 36 League games and Morton finished a full 14 points ahead of second-placed Clyde (in the days when only two points were awarded for a win).

Danny Ferguson was signed after playing briefly in South Africa and lengthily for Heart of Midlothian. A strong right-back, he was a fearless competitor. His football career began with Ormiston Primrose before Hamilton and then Hearts signed him up. He scored Hearts' 5,000th League goal.

Tommy Coakley was a tricky winger who played for Motherwell when only sixteen. He played with Arsenal and then Detroit before joining Morton. He later managed Walsall with considerable success.

A mid-1960s team group, possibly pictured at Stenhousemuir. The players are from left to right, back row: Boyd, Mallon, Brown, Reilly, Kiernan, Strachan. Front row: Adamson, Stevenson, Caven, McGraw, Wilson.

Throughout the 1960s, Annfield was home to Stirling Albion. In this study Morton are on the defensive as the Stirling forwards press for a goal – note the Ochil Hills in the background, surely one of the most scenic views in British football.

October 1965 and this ageing photograph shows Morris Stevenson scoring for Morton at a packed Tannadice Park against Dundee United. The newspaper of the day has slightly doctored the picture to suit the needs of a sports photograph.

A trip to Kirkcaldy in the 1960s with Joe Mason in white on the Raith goal line. The game was played at Stark's Park.

'The Real Madrid effect' – Morton pictured in all white. From left to right, back row: Smith, Gray, Laughlin, Sorensen, Strachan, Bartram, Thorup, Murray. Front row: -?-, Sweeney, Kennedy, Stevenson, Arentoft, Mason.

The League Cup provided Morton with some glorious adventures in the 1960s. Here a packed Cappielow sees Bobby Adamson hover over the Motherwell goalkeeper Peter McCloy. Note the enclosure in front of the main stand at Cappielow. Morton won this game 2-0 to reach the semi-finals.

One of the great occasions in the history of Morton was the epic League Cup Semi-final battle with Hibernian. The first game produced a 1-1 draw and Morton won the replay 1-0 at Ibrox.

There was to be no repeat of the 1922 Scottish Cup Final success in 1963. Rangers won 5-0 to ensure Morton's first ever League Cup Final appearance was a memorable one.

Super sixties striker Allan 'Quick Draw' McGraw.

Two fine action shots of Morton on the attack at the Sinclair Street End of Cappielow.

Joe Mason thunders home a goal under the lights at Cappielow. Mason had been signed from Kilmarnock in 1966 and proved himself an able finisher and quite a creative player too. Indeed, his stylish play was rewarded in the early seventies when Rangers signed him.

Chewing gum cards were popular with schoolboys throughout the 1960s. The card here shows Joe Mason and the text on the back reveals that he played with Lugar Boswell Thistle in the Ayrshire Junior ranks before joining Kilmarnock. He then moved to Morton in 1966 and was with the 'Ton until his transfer to Rangers.

A perfect example of the 'man in black', as Morton goalkeeper Eric Sorensen was known in his early days. From left to right, back row: Boyd, Laughlin, Sorensen, -?-, Smith, Strachan. Front row: Harper, Stevenson, Gray, McGraw, -?-.

In 1968 Morton were in the Scottish Cup Semi-finals. They got there by beating Highland League Elgin City in the quarter-finals at Cappielow. A packed crowd saw the Greenock men edge home 2-1 – Joe Mason, despite being the only Morton player in the picture, has just scored the winner.

By the late 1960s the Morton programme had begun to improve considerably. A feature of this era were the distinctive cover designs. Here the Greenock Town Hall is displayed prominently on a League match programme.

The Cloch Lighthouse and the Argyll Hills featured for a season and caught the Tail o'the bank theme perfectly.

FIXTURES & RESULTS

Scottish League Cup — Section 6.

1966.			F.	A.	Goal Scorers
Aug. 13—East Fife	... ...	(H)	2	1	Borthwick, Gray.
„ 17—Third Lanark	... ...	(A)	1	0	Mason.
„ 20—Arbroath	... ...	(A)	0	0	
„ 27—East Fife	... ...	(A)	1	0	Mason.
„ 31—Third Lanark	... ...	(H)	3	2	Harper, Mason, Stevenson.
Sept. 3—Arbroath	... ...	(H)	2	0	Stevenson, Mason.
„ 5—Brechin City	... ...	(A)	2	1	Mason, Stewart.
„ 7—Brechin City	... ...	(H)	5	2	Bolton, Mason (2), Arentoft, Gray.
Quarter Final:					
„ 14—Aberdeen	... ...	(H)	3	1	Mason (2), Gray.
„ 21—Aberdeen	... ...	(A)	0	3	

League Championship

Aug. 24—Stenh'muir	... ...	(A)	4	1	Ewing, Mason (2), Arentoft.
Sept. 10—Cowdenbeath	... ...	(A)	1	0	Mason
„ 14—Brechin City	... ...	(A)	P		
„ 17—E. Stirling	... ...	(H)	4	0	Mason (2), Harper, Arentoft.
„ 24—Third Lanark	... ...	(A)	1	1	Mason.
„ 28—Brechin City	... ...	(H)	4	1	Bolton, Mason (2), Harper (Pen).
Oct. 1—Clydebank	... ...	(H)	6	0	Borthwick (3), Mason, Gray, Harper.
„ 4—Stenhousemuir	...	(H)	9	1	Bolton (4), Mason (2), Harper (2), Borthwick
„ 8—Raith Rovers	...	(H)	1	0	Bolton.
„ 15—Queen of South	...	(A)	5	2	Mason (3), Bolton (2).
„ 22—Albion Rovers	...	(H)	2	1	Mason, Harper (Pen).
„ 29—Alloa	... ...	(A)	1	0	Mason.
Nov. 5—Forfar Ath.	...	(H)	3	0	Harper, Mason, Bolton.
„ 12—Berwick Rangers	...	(A)	4	1	Harper (2) (1 pen), Loughlan, Mason.
„ 22—Queen's Park	...	(H)	5	0	Harper (2), Arentoft (2), Bolton.
„ 26—Dumbarton	... ...	(A)	1	0	Stevenson.
Dec. 3—East Fife	... ...	(H)	2	1	Harper, Mason.
„ 10—Stranraer	... ...	(A)	3	1	Harper (3).
„ 17—Montrost	... ...	(H)	7	0	Harper (2) (1 pen.), Mason (2), Stevenson, Gray, Ewing.
„ 24—Arbroath	... ...	(A)	0	0	
„ 26—Third Lanark	...	(H)	6	0	Stevenson (2), Harper (2) (1 pen.), Mason (2)
„ 31—Hamilton	... ...	(A)	2	1	Mason, Harper.
1967.					
Jan. 2—Cowdenbeath	...	(H)	0	2	
„ 3—E. Stirling	... ...	(A)	2	1	Boyd, Harper.
„ 14—Clydebank	... ...	(A)	1	0	Harper.
„ 21—Raith Rovers	...	(A)	1	0	Mason.
„ 28—Clyde	(H)				
(Scot. Cup 1st Rd.)					
Feb. 4—Queen of South	...	(H)			
„ 11—Albion Rovers	...	(A)			
„ 18—Scottish Cup 2nd Rounl.					
„ 25—Alloa	... ...	(H)			
Mar. 4—Forfar Ath.	...	(A)			
„ 11—Berwick R.	...	(H)			
„ 18—Queen's Park	...	(A)			
„ 25—Dumbarton	... ...	(H)			
Apr. 1—East Fife	... ...	(A)			
„ 8—Stranraer	... ...	(H)			
„ 15—Montrose	... ...	(A)			
„ 22—Arbroath	... ...	(H)			
„ 29—Hamilton	... ...	(H)			

In season 1967/68 Morton achieved promotion with ease, not to mention a glut of goals. The results page from the match programme shows that the two Joe's (Mason and Harper) were amongst the goals.

Hugh Strachan, a wing half who was signed from Motherwell in 1963, was a remarkably consistent performer.

Contrasting strips for first and reserve team players as Morton prepare for another season in July 1968.

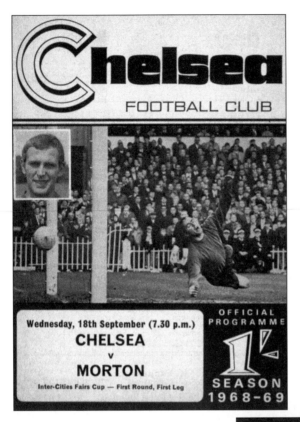

Into Europe! Well, to be precise England. In season 1968/69 Morton competed in the Inter-Cities Fairs Cup (the predecessor of the UEFA Cup) but instead of drawing exotic foreign opponents they came up against English side Chelsea. Beaten 5-0 at Stamford Bridge the club bowed out 8-3 on aggregate.

George Anderson was with Port Glasgow when he joined Morton in 1970. He made his debut as a sixteen-year-old and went on to play for Scotland at Under-23 level. A short stint at Airdrie was followed by his return to Morton. A hard and powerful central defender, he was a regular during his Morton career.

In May 1968 the Scottish Schools Football Association selected Cappielow Park for the annual Scotland v. Wales fixture. The award of this fixture was as much recognition for the steady stream of talent to emerge from Greenock Schools' Football as any preference for Cappielow Park. In the past Greenock schools had given both Charlie Cooke and Tommy Bryceland to senior football.

In the summer of 1969, Morton reached the Scottish Cup Semi-final. Unfortunately, they ran into an on-form Celtic and lost 4-1. Here Leif Neilsen gets down to foil Celtic's Stevie Chalmers. Within a few years Chalmers would be swapping the green and white hoops of Celtic for the blue and white hoops of Morton.

The 1969/70 season is just around the corner on this gloriously sunny day. Note the huge crane dominating the industrial skyline in the background. The Renfrewshire Cup is the larger of the two trophies on display.

Five

Viking Invasion

The Danish invasion of Cappielow Park in the mid-1960s was largely the work of Hal Stewart. Like many successful stories it began almost by accident. Danish players were amateurs and this meant that in essence they were free agents. Any club wishing to sign a Danish player had therefore to merely meet the player's own personal terms. However, a Danish professional player in the early sixties was not eligible to play for Denmark, so Danish players on the whole were reluctant to dabble with professional football. They therefore represented a marvellous untapped market.

Of course, some Danes had travelled abroad to further their careers. Morton were not the first British club by any means to take Danish players, and in 1948 Hull City had signed the Danish internationalist Viggo Jensen who remained on Humberside long enough to amass over 300 League appearances.

What made the Morton experience unique is the fact that the club went back time and time again to recruit Danes and eventually even took Danish players from countries other than Denmark. Hal Stewart was astute and often signed his Scandinavian players in plush Glasgow Hotel rooms, thereby creating an image of swank and substance that Cappielow could never have mustered. But his real coup was in selling the players on to other British clubs and bringing in vital transfer fees.

Erik Sorensen: Signed in March 1962 from Odense, this nineteen-year-old Danish goalkeeper was one of the finest Hal Stewart signings. Remarkably, his transfer was a fluke. Stewart actually wanted to sign another Danish goalkeeper but was advised to sign Sorensen instead. Erik played a trial against Third Lanark in all-black and when Morton refused to name him he was dubbed 'the man in black' or 'Mr X'. He was sold to Rangers for £25,000 in July 1967 but later returned to the club. Moreover, he was Morton manager for a short spell in the early 1970s.

Kai Johansen (left) was a classy full-back who joined the club shortly after Eric Sorensen. Strong in the tackle and purposeful when going forward, he was eventually sold to Rangers in June 1965 for £20,000. In 1966 he had the distinction of scoring the winning goal in the Scottish Cup Final.

Leif Nielsen joined Morton in 1969 from Houston All
Stars in Texas. He joined Morton with thirty-four Danish
caps already to his name. Sadly, this talented goalkeeper
suffered a bad leg-break at Kilmarnock and this effectively
shortened his career. He is on the extreme left of the
above group.

Bjarne Jensen was a right half who was signed from
Aarhus. He was a fairly useful goalscorer and hit a hat-
trick against Stirling Albion in one of his finest displays.

Flemming Neilson was the most high profile of Morton's Scandinavian signings. Recruited from Atalanta of Italy, he was out of contract and had played for the Italian League against the Scottish League at Hampden shortly before joining Morton. His time in Greenock was spent as a sweeper and his creativity was much admired. He could speak six languages and, standing at over six feet tall, was a most impressive man.

Preben Arentoft was an athletic player who was already a Danish internationalist when he joined Morton. Signed from Bronshoj in 1965, he was later sold to Newcastle United and scored for them in the Fairs City Cup Final. He eventually finished his professional career with Blackburn Rovers. In this photograph he is on the steps of the bus with John Madsen behind him. Here, Mr R. Aitken and Mr A. Banks are presenting Erik Sorensen with a pamphlet about the Morton Overseas Club.

Carl Bertelsen in one of those carefully staged photographs which were beloved of sports photographers in the mid-sixties. Note the telegraph pole like structure holding the Cappielow floodlights up. Club secretary Tom Robertson travelled with Hal Stewart to see Bertelsen and they were quick to snap up the pacy striker. He was sold on to Dundee in 1965 and later played with Kilmarnock. His claim to fame in Greenock is being the 'scorer' of the last minute 'goal' at Parkhead in January 1965 that never was. Apparently the referee had already blown for time and the goal was chalked off enabling Celtic to escape with a 3-3 draw.

John Madsen was signed by Morton in 1965 and subsequently transferred to Hibernian. He was only 5'10" but a solid centre-half nevertheless. Known as something of a 'hard man' in the Danish game, he proved himself both quiet and classy. He lost his international status by joining Morton.

Borge Thorup was signed from Bronshoj of Denmark in 1966. Sold to Crystal Palace in 1969, he later returned to Greenock and settled in the area, living near Hunter's Quay and working on the local ferry service.

Per Bartram was an unorthodox Danish centre forward who already owned ten Danish international caps when he joined Morton in 1967. On 28 April 1969 he scored a hat-trick against Celtic at Parkhead in a 4-2 win. He was ultimately sold to Crystal Palace.

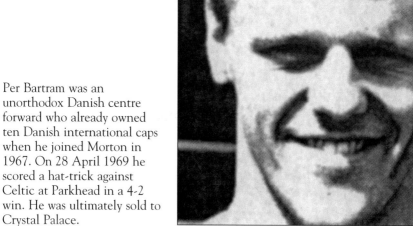

Jorn Sorensen had thirty-one Danish caps when he was signed from Metz of France. Signed for £15,000 he made his debut in a friendly at Coventry and scored in a 2-2 draw. In August 1965 he moved to Rangers with Craig Watson coming to Morton in part-exchange. As one Morton supporter noted at the time 'If it goes on like this, we will have to go to Ibrox to watch Morton!'

Kenny Skovdam was signed by Erik Sorensen in 1974 and was described by many as a delicate player with all the Scandinavian skills. He also was reputed to pack a powerful shot. His Cappielow debut came against Aberdeen and was one to remember as he scored in a 3-1 win.

INTRODUCING THE MORTON PLAYERS . . . .

LIEF NIELSEN—Goalkeeper. 6 ft., 12 st. 7 lbs. Joined Morton during the season from Houston All Stars in Texas. Has rapidly gained popularity by his all round brilliance. Is known to our own Kai Johansen and Erik Sorensen as he possesses 34 Danish caps.

DANNY FERGUSON—Right-back. 5 ft. 9 ins., 11 st. 10 lbs. Another Hal Stewart signing Ferguson who was an established Hearts player left for a short spell in South Africa. Strong in the tackle he makes intelligent use of the ball and is a bulwark in the Morton defence.

JIM KERR—Left-back. 5 ft. 8 ins., 11 st. 3 lbs. Jim is known as the "Hamper Boy" at Cappielow. He made his debut against Dundee United at Tannadice in the Scottish Cup and played an important part in Morton's victory. This boy who is only 18 years of age joined Morton from Lochend United appears to have a promising football career.

BJARNE JENSEN—Right-half. 5 ft. 11 ins., 12 st. 4 lbs. This strong limbed Dane from Aarhus who joined Morton as a forward has rapidly established himself as a wing-half. The assertive free running Dane has scored several vital goals for Morton and our players will require to pay particular attention to him.

WILLIAM GRAY—Centre-half. 5 ft. 11 ins., 12 st. Distinguished himself with St. Mirren before making the short journey from Paisley in 1965. A dependable centre-half who is alive to a chance in suddenly switching from defence to brisk attack. Good in the air. Can be menacing at corner-kicks.

HUGH STRACHAN—Left-half. 5 ft. 10 ins., 11 st. When he was released by Motherwell in 1963, Hal Stewart stepped in and signed him, a move I am sure he has never regretted. Strachan operates with dash and understanding from the half-back line, versatile type of player, does not hesitate if he detects an avenue to goal.

JOE HARPER—Outside-right. 5 ft. 8 ins., 11 st. 6 lbs. Joe left Cappielow for £35,000 fee when he joined Huddersfield. Has been a great success since he rejoined the Greenock club. He was in Scotland's Round the World Tour last season and his goal-scoring feats have made him one of the most menacing Greenock attackers.

WILLIAM ALLAN—Inside-right. 5 ft. 8 ins., 11 st. 4 lbs. Since his return from Durban City in 1967 he has underlined the value of his wide experience and ability in snatching a goal chance. Has been unlucky with injuries this season but since his return to fitness has caught the eye with his artistry.

JOE MASON—Centre-forward. 5 ft. 8 ins., 10 st. 12 lbs. Since coming from Kilmarnock in 1966 he has netted many spectacular goals and has always been a menace to our defence. Good in the air. He is one who will be carefully watched today by our defence.

GERRY SWEENEY—Inside-left. 5 ft. 9 ins., 11 st. 7 lbs. Since joining Morton in 1966 from Renfrew Juniors has proved his versatility by playing in every position except goal for the Greenock club. Industrious, intelligent inside-forward who is ever ready to shoot a goal.

PER BARTRAM—Outside-left. 6 ft., 12 st. Another Dane who possesses ten international caps. Joined Morton two years ago. Versatile type of player adventurous and enterprising. Completely unorthodox he wanders all over the forward line looking for a chance.

Player profiles from a 1969 Rangers *v.* Morton programme highlight the Scandinavian influence in the club.

Gudgeir Leifsson was recruited from Icelandic football at twenty-three years of age. By the time he joined Morton in 1975 he had already won twenty-four caps. Sadly, he failed to settle with Morton.

Six

The Sensational Seventies

If Hal Stewart wrote his name largely on the history of Morton in the 1960s, then the same is true of Benny Rooney in the 1970s. His ability to get the best out of the club when operating with part-time players should never be under-estimated.

In the early seventies the club was stagnating near the foot of the First Division and the inevitable relegation would have come in 1975 but for league reconstruction. Sent into the newly created 'middle' league, the club was able to regroup. With Benny Rooney as manager they flourished. In 1977 the stirrings of a new look team were visible and in 1978 Morton won the First Division ahead of the wealthier Hearts and Dundee. To survive in a cut-throat 'Top Ten' in season 1978/79 was remarkable as was the repeat performance in 1979/80.

If the plaudits went to Rooney and his organisation and tactics, then the bouquets went to the one extrovert Morton cherished – Andy Ritchie. Andy was a unique footballer. A wing wizard, a dead-ball expert, a great unpredictable. To look at, he was surely too large and too gangly to cut the ice at the top level. However, on the field he was magnificent and moreover one of the great entertainers in Scottish Football. He won the Scottish Player of the Year award in 1979, a rare accolade indeed for a player not with a big-city club.

The Morton squad that got another decade underway. From left to right, back row: Ian Campbell, Billy Osborne, Billy Gray, Lief Neilson, Billy McDermitt, Denis Laughton, Stan Rankin, Joe Jordan, Joe Mason. Front row: Tommy Coakley, Ernie Hannigan, George McNeill, John Murray, George Anderson, John Lavelle, Gerry Sweeney.

Morton at Wembley! Yes, it's true. In 1971 Morton played in the *Daily Express* Five-a-side Championship at the Empire Pool, Wembley. Here we see Joe Mason in action against West Ham United. Morton were twice successive Scottish Five-a-side champions.

OFFICIAL PROGRAMME **6ᵈ**

SEASON 1970-71

TEXACO

MORTON v WOLVES
Cappielow Park   Wednesday
21st October Kick-Off 7·30 p.m.

Morton took part in the first ever Texaco Cup in 1970. The competition drew together clubs from Scotland, England and Ireland. Amongst the clubs Morton faced were Wolves and West Bromwich Albion. Later the Anglo-Scottish Cup replaced the Texaco, and Morton found themselves up against clubs such as Oldham and Notts County.

Hal's Heroes

OSBORNE MAKES IT MORTON GLORY NIGHT

Express Staff Reporter

West Bromwich Albion ...... 0, Morton ...... 1 (H.T. 0—1)
(Aggregate 1—3)
SCORER: Osborne (20min.).

MAGNIFICENT Morton out-manoeuvred, out-fought and finally humbled their English rivals in the Texaco Cup at The Hawthorns last night.

A goal up from the first leg, Hal Stewart's heroes handed out two lessons to West Brom. In the first half they set an example in skilful attacking play that had their opponents bewildered. And in the second period when they switched to defence they were still clearly in command of the situation.

It was centre forward Billy Osborne who settled it in the 20th minute.

Collins started the move with a perfect pass out to Mason on the right. The inside man lifted the ball across and there was Osborne leaping in the air to head home just beneath the bar.

Two minutes earlier the centre could have done exactly the same from a Hannigan cross, but he was a fraction off target and the ball grazed the bar.

The prompting of Hannigan and the all-action of Sweeney baffled West Brom in a first-half that was largely one-way. Only "Anglo" Bobby Hope, looked as though he might lift his side.

Tactics

The nearest West Brom came to scoring was when Brown got in a storming header near the interval. But Neilsen flung himself across goal to turn the ball away.

The Scots switched their tactics when Rankin, who dislocated a shoulder, was replaced at the interval by Jordan. And they were just as impressive in defence. Bill Gray, in particular, tamed Jeff Astle, England's World Cup leader, and Sweeney continued to stand out in his hard-working role.

Just for good measure, Morton broke away in the closing stages, and Osborne twice hammered the ball against the body of Cumbes, the West Brom keeper, when he could have scored. Then Mason brought the house down with a 30-yard shot which had Cumbes scrambling across his goal, failing to reach the ball which was only inches wide.

West Brom had neither the attacking skill nor the defensive solidity of the Scots.

Ten minutes from time they brought on Lovett for Merrick, but it was far too late to change the shape of the game. Morton had it all sewn up.

WEST BROM — Cumbes; Minton, Merrick; Brown, Talbut, Kaye; McVitie, Suggett, Astle, Hope, Hartford. Subs: Osborne, Lovett.
MORTON — Nielsen; Murray, McDerment; Sweeney, Gray, Rankin; Hannigan, Collins, Osborne, Mason, O'Neill. Subs: Jordan, Sorenson.
Referee—J. Homewood, Sunbury-on-Thames.
Attendance: 16,000.

Morton's 1-0 win over West Bromwich Albion at the Hawthorns was one of their finest ever performances and secured a 3-1 aggregate victory. Albion had men such as Tony Brown, Colin Suggett and Jeff Astle in their ranks but were still no match for the Greenock club.

Gerry Sweeney was originally with Celtic. He joined Morton in the late sixties and played with considerable verve until being sold to Bristol City for £20,000 in August 1971. He gave the Bristol club excellent service too.

Aberdeen have often been uncomfortable at Cappielow. They lost this November 1973 clash 2-0 and here Graham Thomas is applauded by Billy Osborne after the youngster had opened the scoring.

The Greenock Morton Football and Athletic Club Ltd

Centenary Dinner

Monday 21st October 1974

Chairman — PETER SCOTT, M.B.E.

The Tontine Hotel
Ardgowan Square, Greenock

1974 saw Morton celebrate their centenary. A Centenary Dinner in Greenock was just one of the features of the year and one fan had the presence of mind to hang on to a unique souvenir.

The men who took Morton into season 1974/75. Recognised first team players wore the new blue and white striped jersey whilst reserves and youth were kitted out in the Aston Villa style jerseys. From left to right, back row: Anderson, Ewing, Skovdam, Dennison, Hazel, Taylor, Reid, Wilson, Hayes. Middle row: Eric Sorensen (Manager), Lynn, Ritchie, Parker, Nelson, Baines, Kelly, Murray, I. Thomson, Rankin, Gibson, Osborne. Front row: T. Leneghan (Physio), Warwick, O'Donnell, Hegarty, Brown, Hepburn, Hunter, Townsend, Irvine, McGhee, Scobie, McCallion, Barr, McNeil. 'Sugar' Osborne in the middle row, extreme right, later worked for a local coach firm which provided Morton's matchday transport, with Sugar at the wheel!

Jim Townsend was a shrewd midfielder who had played with St Johnstone, Middlesbrough and Hearts before joining his home town club in Greenock.

Davie Hayes was known as an orthodox full back but in the top picture at Airdrie's Broomfield Park he is about to score. The bottom picture was taken at Hamilton Accies' now-destroyed Douglas Park and shows Davie in more defensive duties.

Pictured in front of the main stand preparing for the onset of another season. From left to right, back row: Hal Stewart (Chairman), Neil McNab, George Anderson, Billy Osborne, Alan Johnstone, Roy Baines, John McNamee, Denis Laughton, Steve Ritchie, Stan Rankin, Jim Townsend. Front Row: Neil Murray, Davie Hayes, Hugh McIllmoyle, John Lavelle, Graham Thomas, John Clark, Neil McFarlane.

Neil McNab shows a sense of the shape of football fashion to come by sporting white boots for this team picture. From left to right, back row: Murphy, -?-, Osborne, Anderson, Fallon, Rankin, Laughton, Gillies, Shevlane. Front row: Hayes, Veitch, Lumsden, Chalmers, Mason, McNab, Clark, Smith.

The one and only Joe Jordan. Signed in 1968 from Blantyre Victoria, who had been Junior Cup finalists, he was initially an inside left. He scored early in his career against Partick Thistle and was a regular marksman in the reserves. However, Joe played but a handful of games for Morton in the early seventies before being sold to Leeds United. Thereafter he became one of the most feared strikers in Europe, starring with Leeds, Manchester United, AC Milan and, of course, Scotland. He scored in the final stages of three consecutive World Cups for Scotland.

Willie McLean sits proudly at the front of this team group showing off the First Division Championship trophy. To his left is Jim Holmes and to his right is Jim Duffy.

Jim Holmes. A gifted defender, Holmes was fair, industrious and extremely skilful. Hibernian tried to sign him in the late 1970s.

Davie Hayes. The long-term partner of Jim Holmes, Hayes was a doggedly determined full-back who always gave 100 per cent. Immensely popular, he held the Morton appearance record until it was surpassed by goalkeeper David Wylie.

Joe McLaughlin. A powerful, young centre half, Joe was a fine example of the Morton 'sell-to-survive' policy of the 1970s. Capped by Scotland at Under-21 level, he was ultimately sold to Chelsea for a six-figure sum. He returned to Scotland to end his career and served Falkirk, Hibernian and Clydebank. Joe is seen here shadowing Hearts striker Derek O'Connor.

An aerial duel at Cappielow with Joe McLaughlin pressuring the Notts County defence in an Anglo-Scottish Cup tie.

John McNeil was slight of frame but a useful finisher and clever player. He very nearly joined Dundee United in the 1980s. The picture above is from a Scottish Cup tie at Cappielow in 1981 when Morton defeated Alex Ferguson's Aberdeen 1-0.

Mark McGhee was Morton's prize asset in the mid-1970s. He was a marvellous finisher and it was little surprise when he was sold to Newcastle United. He later served Aberdeen, Celtic and Scotland, and enjoyed a stint playing in Germany. Upon hanging up his boots he entered football management and Reading, Leicester and Wolves all enjoyed his stewardship, although failure to lead the latter to promotion proved his undoing.

Neil Orr had a proud Morton heritage. His father was the Morton legend Tommy Orr who graced Morton's colours with distinction. Young Neil was a defender of some class and made a big-money move to West Ham United. He finished his career in Scotland pulling on the colours of Hibernian and local rivals St Mirren.

In 1978 the popular Tom McNeill (left) was Morton's Player of the Year. Many, however, would argue that the real hero of the season was manager Benny Rooney (extreme right).

Morton were back in the Premier League for season 1978/79. From left to right, back row: Andy Ritchie, Roddy Hutchison, David Rae, Denis Connaghan, Billy Trench, Jim Liddell, Bobby Russell, Ally Scott, Bobby Thomson. Middle row: Lindsay Hamilton (Physio), Jim McLean, Neil Orr, Charlie Brown, Barry Evans, Joe McLaughlin, Jim Wilkie, Jim Tolmie, Jim Rooney, Billy Thomas, Eamonn Lynch, Willie Gray (Trainer). Front row: Mike Jackson (Assistant Manager), Jim Homes, Jimmy Miller, Tommy Veitch, John McNeil, Benny Rooney (Manager), David Hayes, Allan McKeeman, Danny Docherty, Norman Sutton, Allan McGraw (First Team Coach).

The legendary Jock Stein selected two Morton players for this Scottish League side in 1978. Stein himself is on the extreme right of the back row standing next to Morton's very own legend, Andy Ritchie. In the front row Jim Tolmie, sporting the obligatory perm, is on the extreme left. Second from the right on the front row is Jackie McNamara, who followed up a long career with Hibernian by joining Morton. Amongst others in the picture are Ally MacLeod (front row, third from the right), Billy Thomson (the goalkeeper to the right) and Dougie Somner (second from the left in the back row), all of whom played for Morton's fierce local rivals St Mirren.

Andy Ritchie arrived from Celtic and was soon known as the ambling giant. His ungainly and apparently lazy style masked some quite extraordinary skills – but not for long. Ritchie at his peak was a mesmerizing player and scored some quite stunning goals for Morton. Here he is in action against Notts County under the lights at Cappielow.

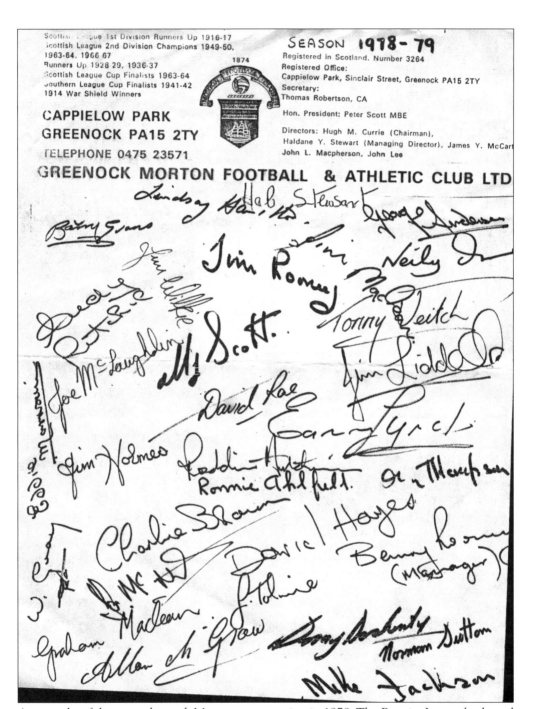

Autographs of the men who took Morton to promotion in 1978. The Premier League beckoned for the likes of Joe McLaughlin, Neil Orr, Jim Holmes, Davie Hayes and the mercurial Andy Ritchie.

DINNER

THURSDAY, 3rd AUGUST, 1978

* * *

To mark the achievement of the

GREENOCK MORTON
FOOTBALL AND ATHLETIC CLUB

in winning the
Scottish First Division Championship
and
Reserve League Championship
Season 1977-78

* * *

Chairman .... Provost A. O. Fletcher

Printed by Orr, Pollock & Co. (Printers) Ltd., 2 Crawfurd Street, Greenock

The achievement of promotion was marked by a dinner in Greenock. The evening was chaired by Provost Freddie Fletcher, who would later make quite a name for himself at Newcastle United. Fletcher, Hal Stewart, Benny Rooney, Allan McGraw and Mike Jackson all signed the menu card.

Benny Rooney has his charges all set for another testing campaign. Note Allan McGraw was the youth coach – he is on the extreme left of the middle row, next to Andy Ritchie.

Bobby Russell was a key player in Morton's Championship-winning team of 1978. Signed from Alloa for £10,000, he scored on his debut and settled very quickly.

Jimmy Miller cost £10,000 from Motherwell in February 1978 and bolstered the Morton midfield. Whilst Andy Ritchie had the flair, Miller had the drive and industry to complement the 'Idle Idol'. What Miller lacked was a goal-threat, but Ritchie took care of that!

A powerful looking Morton squad. From left to right, back row: Holmes, Rooney, Millar Baines, Ritchie, Melville Anderson, Hutchison, Scott. Front row: McNeill, Orr, McLaughlin, Thomson, Wilkie, McLaren, Tolmie.

Roy Baines was born in Derby and signed for County as a youngster. However, it was two seasons with Hibernian that got his senior career underway. He joined Morton in 1972 and learned much under the guidance of Erik Sorensen. Sold to Celtic when Andy Ritchie joined Morton, he later rejoined at Cappielow.

Jim Tolmie crashes in a shot against Celtic in 1981. Tolmie was a clever player whose strength belied a slight frame. He later starred with Lokeren in Belgium and Manchester City, before coming home to Morton to finish his career in the 1980s.

Dundee United manager Jim McLean was a long-term admirer of Morton forward John McNeill (left) but could never quite make up his mind to take the plunge. He got his man briefly, however, by swapping Ian Gibson (right) to Morton on a short-term deal.

Andy Ritchie was deadly from free-kicks and capable of carving defences open with a sway of his hips or a subtle dummy. He became an icon at the club and a free-kick within shooting distance was viewed like a penalty by Morton fans. He was voted the Players' Player of the Year in 1978. Here he prepares for a free-kick in a match against St Mirren in 1981 with some relish, whilst John McNeil makes a point to the referee.

Bad-boy Bobby Thomson? Thomson joined Morton from St Johnstone and had innumerable brushes with authority thanks to a temper which was both swift and purposeful. He was eventually sold to Middlesbrough but not before he was sent off twice in the same game following an infamous run-in with Rangers' Sandy Jardine in a vital Premier Division clash at Cappielow.

The men who fell out. A packed Cappielow looks on as Thomson outjumps Jardine with John McNeil awaiting any scraps. The ball would be secondary to the action later as Thomson and Jardine 'disagreed'.

Goalmouth thrills and spills here in the late 1970s as Aberdeen keeper Jim Leighton foils Drew Busby in this Morton attack at Cappielow. The Morton player watching from a safe distance is John McNeil.

Andy Ritchie (11) was the master of bending the ball around the wall, but occasionally had to take his turn of preventing the ball going round the wall at the other end. Here, Jim Holmes talks to the Morton goalkeeper as the 'Ton defend a free kick.

In 1979 Morton reached the League Cup Semi-final. Sadly they were dogged by bad-luck on the day and fell 2-1 to Aberdeen at Hampden. Here, former Morton hero Mark McGhee sends Aberdeen on their way with a header. In the background is the dearly departed old North Stand that gave an unrivalled view of proceedings at Hampden Park.

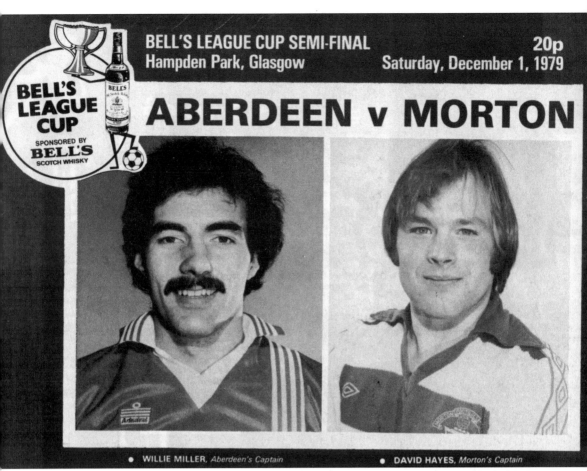

BELL'S LEAGUE CUP SEMI-FINAL
Hampden Park, Glasgow

20p
Saturday, December 1, 1979

ABERDEEN v MORTON

● WILLIE MILLER, *Aberdeen's Captain*   ● DAVID HAYES, *Morton's Captain*

The programme from Morton's 1979 League Cup Semi-final with Aberdeen. The feeling in Greenock was that Benny Rooney's men should have beaten Aberdeen and were the victims of a couple of borderline decisions.

Morton *v.* St Mirren at a packed Cappielow. The Renfrewshire derby between the Greenock and Paisley sides is a highly charged affair in which local pride is at stake.

Seven

Into the Eighties

The departure of Benny Rooney was bound to create a period of uncertainty at Morton. Various managers came in after Rooney and some did very well, notably Tommy McLean and Alex Miller, but each time they were lured away by bigger jobs. What settled Morton was the return of one of it's favourite sons … Allan McGraw.

As a striker McGraw had been peerless for Morton, his scoring exploits outrageous. Now he completed his coaching apprenticeship and became Morton manager. His philosophy was sound. As well as building entertaining teams he continued the 'sell to survive' policy and ensured the club survived into the 1990s.

Relegated in 1983, Morton were promoted in 1984, relegated in 1985 and promoted once more in 1987, only to go down again in 1988. The decade lacked nothing in excitement. There were, of course, a host of fine players too.

This was the Morton squad that lined up for season 1981/82. Bernie Slaven, fourth from the left in the middle row, was to become a sensational goalscorer in England with Middlesbrough, but failed to display that kind of promise in his stay with Morton. By the time he matured into a clinical finisher in England he was well out of Morton's price range. From left to right, back row: Alistair Maitland, Martin Doak, John Marr, Robert Houston, John Reynolds, Joe McLaughlin, Andy Ritchie, Roddie Hutchison. Middle row: Davie Hayes, Liam Kennedy, Steven Murphy, Bernie Slaven, Jim Wilkie, Graham Kyle, Jim Rooney, Eddie Gavigan, Gary Dickie, Eddie McNab, Danny Docherty. Front row: Eddie Morrison, Bjarne Jensen, Jim Holmes, Neil Orr, Bobby Thomson, Mike Jackson, Ian Cochrane, John McNeil, Joe Gillies, Willie Gray (Trainer), Gerry McElhill (Physio).

Panic! The Morton goal is under siege at Cappielow as Rangers press for a goal. The Morton players pictured are Bobby Thomson, 'keeper Roy Baines and Joe McLaughlin. The game ended 2-2.

Morton prepare for another season, this time in the First Division in 1983. The coach on the extreme left of the middle row is Martin Ferguson, brother of the Manchester United manager Alex. It was another Alex, Miller, who was in charge of Morton in 1983, but his stay was all too brief and firstly St Mirren and then Hibernian and Aberdeen utilized his managerial skills. Pictured from left to right, back row: Wilson, Nolan, McDonald, Clinton, McCallum, Armstrong. Middle row: M. Ferguson, Robertson, Duffy, Doak, Kyle, Higgins, Houston, Welsh, McElhill. Front row: Morrison, Holmes, Rooney, McNeil, Miller (Manager), McNab, Clinging, Hayes, Gray. When Miller left to become manager of St. Mirren it was Eddie Morrison who stepped into the breach and the former Kilmarnock striker was the club's third manager in only seven months.

In May 1985 Morton defender Jim Duffy was voted the Scottish Players' Player of the Year. Signed from Celtic, he had never played for the Glasgow club, but at Morton he flourished. He eventually moved on and made a career at Dundee, Partick Thistle and Falkirk. He managed Falkirk and Dundee with some success before finally having an unsuccessful stint as the Hibernian boss.

In March 1988 Morton sold their young starlet Archie Gourlay to Newcastle United. Gourlay was every bit the teenage sensation with an extraordinary range of skills. Alas, he failed to break into the Newcastle United team and even a return to Scotland with Motherwell could not resurrect a career that promised so much at one time.

David Hopkin was one of the most talented players to step into the Morton side in the 1980s. Signed from Port Glasgow Rangers Boys Club, he was to manage just eighteen games for Morton before the inevitable big offer came in. It was Crystal Palace who took the plunge and their bravery was rewarded when David was sold on by the South London club to Leeds United in 1997. In his last game for Crystal Palace he came to national attention when his last minute lob beat the Sheffield United goalkeeper to win the Wembley Play-off Final for Palace. Before he could kick a Premiership ball for Palace he was off to Leeds for £3,250,000. By this stage he could do no wrong and he capped a fine performance for Scotland by scoring twice in a 4-1 win over Belarus at Aberdeen.

In 1985 Morton signed goalkeeper David Wylie from Ferguslie United and he went on to become one of the most loyal servants the club has had. Agile and brave, he was a dependable part of the Allan McGraw term in office and only left the club in the late 1990s after a thoroughly deserved testimonial match. He subsequently played with Clyde.

Rowan Alexander. Born in Ayr, Rowan had played with Queen of the South, St Mirren and Brentford before joining Morton. He proved a prolific marksman at Cappielow. When he left Morton it was to join Queen of the South as player/manager. He is pictured here with the Second Division Championship that Morton won in 1995.

105

A foggy Easter Road with Hibernian defenders stoutly resisting Morton pressure at a corner kick. The huge terracing in the background has long since been reduced in size.

Mark McGraw

Former Morton legend Allan McGraw instilled all of his knowledge in his son Mark. Clearly Mark had a lot to live up to and Hibernian signed him when he had made just a handful of outings for the Greenock side. He later served Falkirk and returned to Morton before a stint with Clyde. His was the strange tale of a son sold by his father!

Former Celtic and Hibs defender Jackie McNamara boosted the Morton defence in the 1980s. A clever player, he was also something of a political activist and was a prominent speaker for the Scottish Socialist Party at the new Scottish Parliament Elections in 1999.

Eight
So near in the Nineties

There was to be no respite for Morton supporters in the 1990s as their emotional strength was tested to the limit. In 1990/91 the club lost a replayed Scottish Cup Quarter-final tie to Motherwell on penalties after outplaying the Lanarkshire club in the first game at Fir Park.

The very next season saw Morton lose another Scottish Cup Quarter-final, this time to Celtic. In the League the club could not escape to the Premier Division – they therefore did the next best thing and were relegated to the Second Division!

Not for the first time in the history of Morton this proved the ideal recipe for recovery. The Second Division was duly won in a canter, with the club sporting natty Blue Tartan strips. Nothing they had done could prepare the fans for the1995/96 season as Morton came within an ace of making it back-to-back promotions.

In a magnificent season for the First Division, Dundee United, Dunfermline and Morton slugged it out for the one automatic promotion spot and single play off position. Then, as the finishing tape neared, St Johnstone joined the fray. The last few weeks of a memorable season had enough heartache and joy to fill a soap opera. In the end Morton failed narrowly and finished up third. A case of so near, yet so far.

Alas, the near thing did not signal the start of anything better and by the late 1990s the club had changed hands and a new broom was sweeping through the club.

Chairman John Wilson sold the club to Hugh Scott and the new man set about rejuvenating the club. Out went manager Allan McGraw and in came Billy Stark. Stark had to contend with rebuilding a side that had lost the likes of McInnes and Lilley but he did so without fuss and his youth policy, in which Peter Weir played a huge role, began to reap dividends. As the new century beckoned the club sought to move out of Cappielow and challenge for a spot in the top league.

As well as playing in the Scottish League and Scottish Cup, Morton have played in a number of other domestic competitions. To celebrate its centenary in 1990 the Scottish League introduced a knockout cup for those clubs not in the Premier Division. It proved highly popular with Dundee winning the final against Ayr United at Fir Park, Motherwell. Indeed so popular was the competition that it was decided to continue it. In its third season, Morton battled through to the Final and met Hamilton Academical at nearby Love Street, Paisley. Sadly, despite two goals from Rowan Alexander, Morton lost a thrilling final 3-2. Even worse, young midfield prodigy Alan Mahood sustained a serious knee injury that would rule him out of action for over a year.

The programme from Hamilton *v.* Morton in November 1993 is worthy of note as the game was abandoned after only seventeen minutes. The problem was snow, which fell with such force that it quickly obscured the lines on the pitch. In blizzard conditions there was no alternative but to abandon the match.

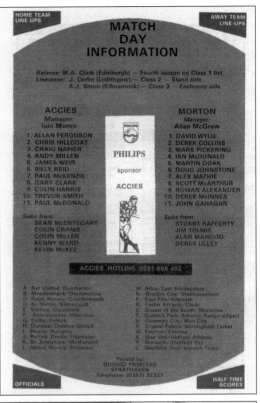

Alex Mathie and Derek McInnes talk to the press on the pitch in front of the Main Stand. In two seasons at Cappielow, Mathie scored 45 goals and at £75,000 from Celtic he was a real bargain. Newcastle United bought him in July 1993 for £250,000. Mathie followed Reid, McGraw, Mahood, Turner and Gourlay in big money moves from Greenock. McInnes, a gifted left-sided midfielder was to follow, joining Rangers in November 1995 for £300,000.

Tea and sympathy for Morton manager Allan McGraw, dispensed here by Janey Rankin. Janey was the club secretary for many years and a popular point of contact with football administrators throughout Scotland.

Martin Doak was awarded a testimonial match by the club when his career was cut short by injury. He joined the club in 1979 as a fifteen-year-old and over the years developed into a fine central defender.

Lindberg and Rajamaki. Morton dabbled in the Scanadinavian transfer market again in 1991 when they recruited Marko Rajamaki (below) and Janne Lindberg (right). Lindberg was a huge success with Morton, and a Finnish internationalist, who linked well with Derek McInnes and Alan Mahood.

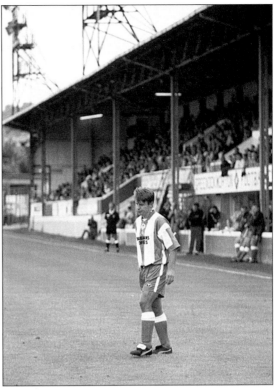

Rajamaki was a tricky winger who scored a healthy number of goals.

Englishman Warren Hawke was a football headline writer's dream. Hawke scored a hat-trick for Berwick against Morton when both clubs were in the Second Division and the club never forgot it. He was duly signed and soon formed a potent striking partnership with Derek Lilley. Hawke had played for Sunderland in a FA Cup Final at Wembley and was more at ease there than with an eagle on his shoulder!

Brian Reid was a towering centre half who impressed with his solid defending and sheer physical presence. His displays soon brought the transfer offers and Rangers snapped him up for £300,000 in March 1991. Tragically, he suffered cruciate ligament damage in a testimonial match and although he hung on, his time at Rangers was effectively over. He returned to Morton and quickly re-established his popularity.

Farewell Cappielow? The 'Wee Dublin' End, so called as it once had an area of prefabricated houses behind it used by Irish immigrants.

The Sinclair Street End. Here the only road access to Cappielow runs alongside the ground. The clock and half-time scoreboard are throwbacks to a pre-electronic scoreboard era.

The lovingly named 'Cowshed.' This covered enclosure has always been the main gathering point for Morton supporters. However, in the late 1970s, as football violence increased, it was initially segregated by hard-worked policemen and finally segregated formally by a high fence. Thereafter, Sinclair Street became the means of access for all Morton supporters.

The Main Stand at Morton dates back to the 1930s and has undergone various reincarnations. The sky-lighting and yellow and blue seats were perhaps the best improvement and initiated by new club owner Hugh Scott in the 1990s.

Occasionally, superstars come to Cappielow. In a pre-season friendly in 1998 with Hearts, the Argentinian striker Balbo was fielded by the Edinburgh club. Balbo had been a prolific marksman in Serie A but found Harry Curran a difficult customer to shake off in Greenock!

PRESENTS

A STAR STUDDED **TRIBUTE DINNER**

TO

Allan McGraw

Glasgow Thistle Hotel, Sunday, 26th October, 1997

7.00 pm for 7.30 pm   CARRIAGES MIDNIGHT   DRESS: LOUNGE SUITS

All proceeds raised go to Variety Club Scotland Childrens Charity

In 1997 the Variety Club had a tribute dinner for Allan McGraw. One of the most popular figures in Scottish football, McGraw had served Morton with distinction, both as a player and as a manager.

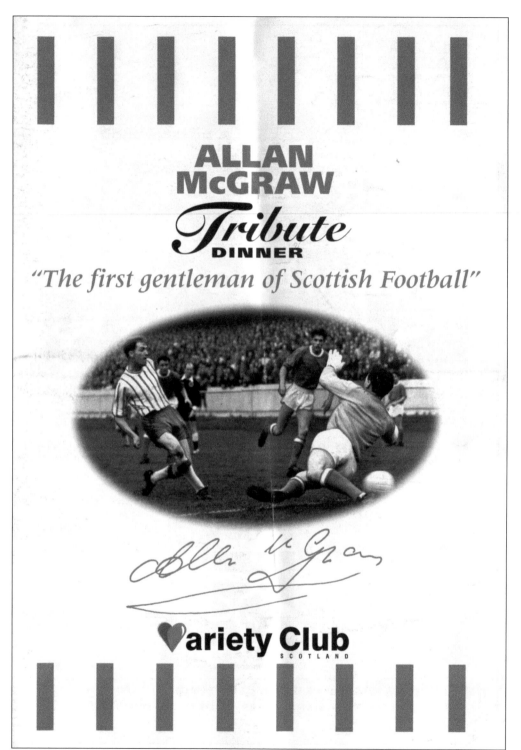

The programme from Allan McGraw's tribute dinner.

Club Mascots. In the 1990s many clubs introduced a club mascot to their pre-match entertainment. In Morton's case a dinosaur was created and given the name 'Mortonosaurous'. Here, he is pictured before a Morton *v.* Raith Rovers clash, with an over-age match mascot who was a notable and humorous departure from the usual schoolboy! The dinosaur was not Morton's first mascot – in the club's earlier days sheep had grazed on Cappielow and one of their number, 'Toby', was the mascot!

Fifers foiled in the final minute

First Division: *Rajamaki header denies Dunfermline in fiery climax to promotion clash*

Greenock Morton   **1**
Rajamaki (90)

Dunfermline   **1**
Millar (50 pen)

HUGH KEEVINS

THE First Division's winning post is not yet in sight for Dunfermline after they were denied victory at Cappielow last night because of an injury-time goal by Greenock Morton's Marko Rajamaki.

Flared tempers added to the eventful climax, when Dunfermline's John Clark clashed with Morton's Derek Collins after the final whistle. Club officials came on to the pitch to separate the players, while the watching referee doubtless took a mental note for his report.

Dunfermline's disappointment was obvious because they had looked set to claim a considerable advantage over their promotion rivals, as a result of Marc Millar's penalty goal.

It was a throw-in from Derek Collins, however, which enabled Finnish internationalist Rajamaki to beat goalkeeper Ian Westwater with a header at the near post.

As a result, the quest for promotion remains unresolved. Only three points separate Dunfermline from Dundee United, and both have played the same number of games.

When they are wearing their away strip, of red and blue quarters, Dunfermline's outfield players resemble jockeys in racing silks.

They were certainly slower out of the stalls and Westwater was required to make three saves, one of them an outstanding stop from a Rajamaki volley, before Dunfermline had broken out of a trot.

However, Dunfermline soon overcame their indifferent start and showed an appetite for testing Davie Wylie.

Andy Smith and Allan Moore forced the goalkeeper to deal with a combination of shots but he was powerless to prevent the visitors from going in front after 50 minutes. Smith was clearly impeded inside the penalty box by Peter Cormack, and Millar made an efficient job of striking the ball low into the bottom left hand corner of the net.

A minute later, Dunfermline scorned a chance to put the outcome beyond doubt when they failed to capitalise on a misplaced pass by Wylie.

The significance of that missed opportunity was underlined in injury time when Rajamaki intervened to keep the promotion race wide open.

Attendance: 3,170

Morton: Wylie, Collins, Johnston, Reid, Mc Cahill, McPherson, Lilley, Mahood, Hawke Cormack, Rajamaki. Subs: McArthur, Blai Boe.

Dunfermline: Westwater, Miller, Millar, Clar Tod, Ireland, Moore, Robertson, Smith, Petrie Shaw. Subs: French, Fleming, Van de Kamp.

Referee: R Orr (Kilbarchan)

How they stand

	P	W	D	L	F	A	Pts
Dunfermline	29	17	6	6	59	31	57
Dundee Utd	29	15	9	5	54	31	54
Morton	29	16	4	9	48	36	52
St Johnstone	29	14	7	8	48	33	49
Dundee	29	13	8	8	46	36	47
St Mirren	29	10	7	12	37	41	37
Airdrie	29	8	10	11	34	41	34
Clydebank	29	8	9	12	32	41	33
Hamilton	29	7	6	16	31	46	27
Dumbarton	29	3	2	24	19	72	11

The 1995 promotion race was an epic. Dunfermline, Dundee United, Morton and St Johnstone all sought promotion and in the final fortnight were involved in some remarkable clashes. A month or so from the end of the season Morton salvaged a point against Dunfermline in controversial fashion after the ball was knocked out of play for an injured Pars player to receive treatment. Morton attacked and scored in the ensuing melee.

Morton fill Cup with pure magic

Greenock Morton 2

Kilmarnock 5

Jonathan Northcroft
at Cappielow

ALLAN McGRAW'S knees are wrecked from playing and management causes his heart to be imperilled. This is the sort of situation that must have his doctor pleading caution but also the kind which keeps football men welded to the game.

The 5-2 margin must appear pretty cosy but Kilmarnock will vouch for it being otherwise. Morton's young footballing side have been surprising us for seasons and they thundered back at their opponents, having lost three goals and a man in the first half. Not until the death did their challenge flicker. This was a terrific and hypnotic tie.

Kilmarnock compel admiration too for coming through this test of their character, particularly after their galling evening against Raith Rovers. Until now they were staring at a knockout end to the season all right but it was of the play-off variety to remain in the Premier Division. Now the Scottish Cup final can be glimpsed.

What is unquestionably Premier quality about Kilmarnock is the partnership of Jim McIntyre and Paul Wright, who teased Morton apart until Wright hirpled off having been butchered in the tackle by Steve McCahill, who was subsequently ordered off.

McIntyre, both strong and sleek, continued impressively alone and John Henry gobbled a fine hat-trick. Henry has glittered with promise since his days at Clydebank and, back against First Division opponents, he dazzled once more.

There must once have been a time, hard though it is to imagine, when football hacks were of a smaller girth, such is the design of the Cappielow press box. You are jammed in like anchovies with a thin slat to write on and bits of girder and roofing obstructing every line of sight. But on days like yesterday, with grand old teams meeting in this antique competition, such features become resonant.

They added to the feeling of history the Cup always brings, as did the classic dynamics here: Morton a bold young team and Kilmarnock, slipping in the division above them, the archetypal fall-guys.

Certainly, within minutes, the fragile habits Kilmarnock have built up this season were apparent. With hardly a boot raised in opposition, Marko Rajamaki was in on goal but Dragoje Lekovic blocked with his legs.

With the Finn a floater around Warren Hawke and Derek Lilley, Kilmarnock coped awkwardly with the extra man up front. But what they lost numerically at the back their colleagues gained when attacking en masse and it proved decisive.

The lively support of Dylan Kerr was important in this effort and likewise the willingness to drop off McIntyre and Wright. However, it was from a set-play that Kilmarnock gained the lead.

Tiny David Bagen swerved in a corner which hardly rose above the level of his own chin. It bent against the post and, though Morton hacked it away to the penalty spot, Henry contrived to lift the ball audaciously into the top corner off the back of a defender.

This took a fair element of technique on Henry's part and it was the midfielder's skill which induced Kilmarnock's second. Taking the ball into the box from the right, he reached an impasse so nudged the ball to the onrushing Wright. A path to the net had been cleared by Henry's carry which Wright exploited with a low shot.

Even at 1-0 Morton had still looked bright-eyed with Lilley turning to curl one at Lekovic and Hawke volleying a lick or two over the bar. But the second winded them and promptly there was a third. McIntyre, a footballer with real poise despite his gangly frame, sneaked the ball from John Anderson out on the right byeline. His cross fell behind the defence and Henry turned the ball in.

Morton fans, foolishly it turned out, began to leave for the pub even though we still hadn't reached half-time. McCahill was to join them, red-carded for a murderous lunge at Wright. "Amputation effort" someone called it, though in truth it was high enough to qualify as decapitation.

What wise counsel could McGraw offer after such a collapse? The argument in these situations is surely 'if they can score three goals in a half so can we'. And, 10 minutes after his half-time counselling and cajoling, Alan Mahood made them think they could. Kilmarnock opened up carelessly when their midfielder took the ball in diagonally from the D of the box and produced a precise shot which easily beat Lekovic in goal.

Kilmarnock failed to learn from this while spirit welled up almost visibly in Morton. Mahood scored a second – heading in a pulled-back cross from Derek Collins – and the game seemed fit to burst. Bobby Williamson's temples flushed dark as he leapt from the dugout.

McIntyre settled it, throwing off his man to score with his left, but only Henry's hat-trick, a far-post header, made Morton cede the issue. In the end, Kilmarnock survived but so does the welter of the Cup.

The Cup has given Morton some of its favourite memories. This match against Kilmarnock had the lot – a stirring fightback, a sending off and goals galore!

The man chosen to replace Allan McGraw was never going to have an easy task. Nevertheless, Billy Stark fitted the bill. Immensely popular, his approachable manner and calm method soon won over the fans. He gradually restructured the playing staff at Morton and brought experienced professionals to the club. His own playing career had been most impressive and his midfield talents were utilized to the full by St Mirren, Aberdeen, Celtic and Kilmarnock.

Coaching the youngsters under Billy Stark was Peter Weir. In his own youth Weir had been an outstanding winger with St Mirren and Aberdeen. Here he is looking on in 1980 as Morton gain a penalty at Cappielow in a Renfrewshire derby.

Alan Mahood was one of the club's most influential players in the 1980s and 1990s. His combative midfield talents earned him a big move to Brian Clough's Nottingham Forest, but he failed to settle under Clough and rejoined Morton. A cruciate ligament injury stalled his career for over a year. However, when fully recovered he regained his former strength and eventually moved to his beloved Kilmarnock as a Bosman signing in1998.

Support at Morton has always been vociferous and this picture shows visiting Morton fans at St Mirren's Love Street stadium for a local derby.

Goal! Billy Stark's Morton side in the late 1990s grab a goal at Cappielow. Note the Main Stand in the background with the new tip-up seats having replaced the traditional benches. In the picture are Owen Archdeacon, Alan Blaikie, Steven Aitken (7), Kevin Twaddle, Brian Reid, Harry Curran and John Anderson.

Kevin Twaddle was the type of dashing, ambling winger who was certain to be a hit at Cappielow. His gangly running disguised a very direct style and he knew how to convert chances. He was also something of a dead-ball expert and reminded many Morton fans of Andy Ritchie.

A cartoon of Kevin Twaddle.

Owen Archdeacon had enjoyed a lengthy career prior to becoming a Morton player. He started his career with Celtic but really hit the heights during a seven-year stint at Barnsley where his attacking wing play was gradually transformed into wing-back duties. A super athlete, he later moved to Carlisle before joining Morton. He made his Morton debut in a 1-0 League win at Dens Park and scored a vital Cup goal against the same opponents in 1999. His brother played for St Mirren and Stranraer and faced Owen in some memorable family jousts.

Peter Duffield struggled to establish himself as a striker in England with Middlesbrough and Sheffield United. However, when Hamilton Accies brought him north they ignited a spark. A prolific marksman, he stunned the Hamilton support with a string of goals and was ultimately sold to local rivals Airdrie. He flourished with Airdrie too, and Raith Rovers were next to use his services. When he joined Morton on a Saturday lunchtime there was little chance to introduce him. However, within hours he had scored twice in the local derby with St Mirren, and as Morton strolled to a 3-0 win, his popularity was sealed. His slightly nomadic career saw him move to Falkirk after a few brief months at Greenock.

Sold to Hibernian in 1999, Derek Collins had given Morton loyal service since signing in July 1987. Derek made his bow against Motherwell in the Premier League and scored his first goal in a sensational 3-2 win over Rangers in 1988. A very reliable player he was composed in defence and fairly adventurous in attack. Capable of playing in midfield, he was a versatile squad member and cost Hibernian in the region of £200,000 when they signed him in 1999 as they pushed for promotion to the Premier League.

Edinburgh-born Keith Wright joined Morton in the late 1990s and came with a wonderful career to his name. He started out with Raith Rovers before joining Dundee in a move that was hardly surprising given his sixty goals in just three seasons. Keith kept up an impressive strike rate on Tayside, forging an irresistible partnership with Tommy Coyne. A boyhood supporter of Hibs, he not surprisingly joined them when Hibernian and Aberdeen subsequently vied for his services. In 1991 he scored in the 'Hibees' League Cup Final success and one year on he added a Scotland cap. Keith returned to Raith in 1997 but a year later the 5'11" striker was signed by Billy Stark as Morton sought an experienced front runner.

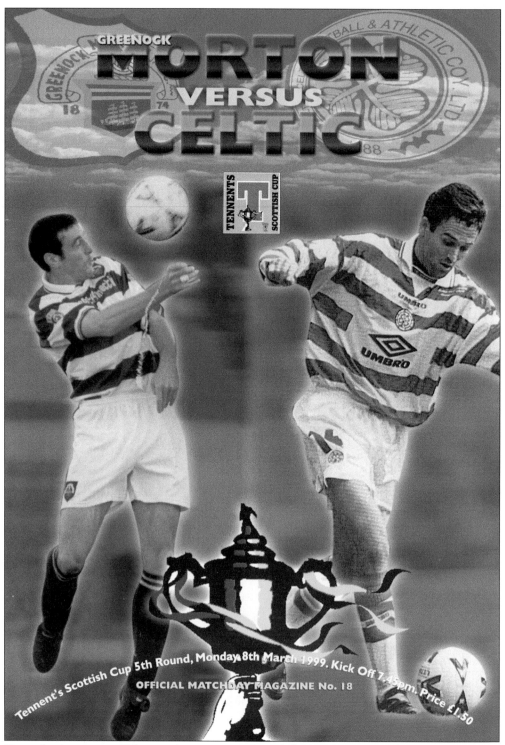

Cappielow's swansong? The match programme from Celtic's visit to Cappielow for the Scottish Cup Quarter-final tie on 8 March 1999.